On the Other Side of the Fence

Edward L. Fandt

VANTAGE PRESS
New York / Washington / Atlanta
Los Angeles / Chicago

FIRST EDITION

Published by Vantage Press, Inc.
516 West 34th Street, New York, New York 10001

Manufactured in the United States of America
ISBN: 0-533-06913-0

Library of Congress Catalog Card No.: 85-91397

The Grass
  Always
    Looks
      Greener . . .

ON THE OTHER SIDE OF THE FENCE

CONTENTS

FOREWORD

On the Other Side of the Fence is a series of vignettes related to our retirement life in the south. These are sketches of factual and semi-factual experiences, slightly embellished with a touch of imagination and humor at times in an effort to prevent boredom and apathy from dominating the narrative.

This is definitely *not* a how-to-do-it book on retirement but strictly a publication which might inspire someone to enjoy some of the challenging potential that exists in the everyday-living events that surround us.

My family, several close friends, and especially my retirement counselor at college were concerned as I approached retirement because of the busy, involved life that I had led for forty-three years. My career as an educator, school administrator and college professor, with leadership roles in various civic and service organizations, had been challenging and quite involved. The concern was that, after looking forward to "life on the other side of the fence"—*retirement*—the sedentary and prosaic life of non-productivity might result in total boredom.

Edward L. Fandt, Ed. D.

ACKNOWLEDGMENTS

To my wife, Mary B. Fandt, who has assisted me in all of my various endeavors during the forty-five years of our married life and who has encouraged and supported me in the wide variety of educational, professional and civic activities in which I have been involved during this time period. She has been a wonderful wife, a loving mother, a steadfast friend, a gracious hostess—who has endured my teasing and repetitious stories with remarkable constraint and who has been inspirational in her support of this literary effort!

To our two daughters, Suellen F. Smith and Patricia M. Fandt, who have, with blind faith in their father, been most supportive and encouraging in this present endeavor.

To my son-in-law, James C. Danos, for his gracious and patient assistance with my computer efforts and his critical analysis of my end products.

To our friends, Thomas F. and Marie Taylor, who were responsible for our move to South Carolina and who have been so helpful to us in our adjustment here.

To a large group of my friends who have endured my writing attempts and, perhaps in desperation, have encouraged me to proceed with this book.

*On the Other Side
of the Fence*

The Natives Were Friendly!

June 16, 1979, was a memorable date for us. We arrived at our new home in South Carolina on the shores of beautiful Lake Hartwell. We had made reservations at a local motel to wait out the arrival of the moving men with our furniture and possessions but when we called our local area friends we were advised to cancel the motel and proceed directly to our new home.

We did, and much to our surprise as we walked in the house, there was a table and two chairs; flowers and dishes and silverware on the table; ice, wine, beer, and food in the refrigerator; pots and cooking utensils on the stove; a king-size mattress and bedding on the floor in the bedroom; soap, towels and toilet paper in the bathrooms—everything ready for us to move in and settle down to normal life!

Since we had made arrangements for the electricity to be turned on and a new refrigerator to be delivered prior to our arrival, we really were in operation immediately—thanks to our friends the Taylors, who had planned with our builder to borrow the house keys and have everything in place for our immediate occupancy.

Yes, Indeed! The natives were friendly!

During the ensuing weeks as we became acquainted with several of the native South Carolinians, we found them to be most gracious and friendly. It just took us some time and repetition of sentences until we began to comprehend some of the local expressions and the "southernese" talk. But then, I suppose that our Yankee speech bothered them just as much.

As we went shopping in the various stores or visited the local restaurants, we were amazed, frankly, at the friendly mannerisms of clerks, storekeepers, waitresses, and other personnel that we encountered. Just everyone seemed to be willing to go out of their way to be helpful.

What a wonderful way to start out our new life in a strange new area!

Over the Water to Swamp Guinea's

On August 1 of our first year of South Carolina residency, our friends Marie and Tom Taylor invited us and our guests, Betty and Mary Loretta Kinney (New Jersey friends of long standing), to accompany them on their pontoon boat to Swamp Guinea's, across the lake in Georgia, for a fish-camp dinner.

Since everyone was agreeable, away we went during early afternoon. With drinks in our hands, it was a relaxing half hour of conversation until we reached the midpoint in the lake. Here, Tom shut off the motor and then went out on the foredeck with his sextant (he was a World War II flyer and navigator) and "shot the sun" to get out exact location. After some calculation, he announced that we were at the junction of the Tugaloo and Seneca rivers at the point where the Savannah River began, and since this constituted the exact border between Georgia and South Carolina, we must comply with the Georgia law which prohibited the bringing of any alcoholic beverage into the state in an open container. Accordingly, we were instructed to finish up our drinks while the South Carolina bottles were being sealed. Obviously, we complied with this mandate and then, as Tom started the boat and we proceeded into Georgia waters, we all volunteered to assist Marie as she opened the bottles of Georgia liquor for consumption on the remainder of the journey.

The boat ride was most enjoyable!—just one unfavorable incident that had possible implications for our homeward trip. While passing under a highway bridge over the Tugaloo River as we were nearing Swamp Guinea's, the riding light on the short mast scraped and broke on the concrete underpart of the bridge. (Tom apologized that he had not calculated the recent rains into the lake, and with the lake up almost two feet, did not have his usual clearance.)

When we arrived at Swamp Guinea's fish camp, four of us Yankees really did not know what to expect! After the boat was tied up we walked into this large building with a series of long benches and newspaper-covered tables. The waitress distributed menus featuring Brunswick stew, chicken wings and thighs, hush puppies, all the catfish you could eat, slaw and rolls, plus other assorted items for those who did not like real catfish eating.

All six of us managed to find something edible—two of our party amazed us as the waitress just kept bringing plates of chicken, catfish, and hush puppies, all of which managed to disappear!

Eventually we finished and made it back to the boat and hurried back to the South Carolina side before darkness set in. There was no stopping as we crossed over the border since it was obvious that there were no alcoholic beverages in open containers—everything was inside us in "skin containers"!

While the food may not have been of the gourmet variety, the outing and the name of the fish camp will always be in our "memorable events" book! Thus, this became one of our first vignettes of our new life and adventures in South Carolina.

3

Up the Cove *with* Only a Paddle!

Some months before we moved to our present location on Lake Hartwell in South Carolina, our daughter Patty and her husband, Jim, took us for a sailboating day at Kerr Lake in North Carolina.

Sailing was a dream come true for me! For years I had watched the sailboats as they quietly skimmed over the water on the lake or ocean and dreamed that some day I would have a sailboat of my own!

At the conclusion of our sailing day, I casually inquired of our daughter as to a "ball-park" figure of the price of a sailboat similar to hers. She gave me an approximate figure which didn't really floor me since I countered with "I'll give you a check in that amount if you ever decide to sell your boat."

Weeks later, shortly after we moved to our new home on Lake Hartwell, Patty and Jim called to advise us that they were coming up from Florida for a visit and an inspection of our new home. You can imagine our surprise when they arrived and pulled into our driveway—trailing the sailboat behind their car. It took only a few minutes of questioning as to why they had brought the boat all the way from Florida—which Patty settled in a hurry with her statement, "Daddy, we're just delivering your boat as per your request!"

A check exchanged hands and I suddenly became a boat owner. The next two days were rather hectic as I was exposed to a series of verbal and written briefings; dry-land instruction and practice on stepping the mast, raising the sails and so on (the weather was too nasty to actually take the boat out on the lake); plus lengthy explanations of the various brochures and manuals that accompanied the sailboat.

After the "young-uns" left for their home, I devoted most of the next two weeks to reviewing all of their oral and written instructions and then tackled the problem of attempting to restore the clamp-on 1.7 hp. gasoline motor to running condition so that I wouldn't end up becalmed out in the middle of the lake. Although I'm not too mechanically inclined, by following the motor manual faithfully, I did manage to get it running in a dry-land test—clamped to a sawhorse, suspended over a large tub of water.

I was ready for my first "a-boating I will go" adventure! A neighbor towed the sailboat to a nearby launching ramp and, wearing my life preserver and equipped with the motor and a paddle in the boat, I began my half-mile water trip to the cove where our house was located.

Some seventy-five feet out from the ramp, I gaily waved to my wife and my friend and attempted to start the motor for the short cruise around to our cove. No success! Again and again I tried—but the motor just would not start! In desperation, I abandoned further efforts with the motor and began to paddle toward the cove. In the meantime, a strong westerly wind developed and, in spite of my paddling efforts, the boat began drifting sideways toward a shoreline covered with huge rocks that the Army Corps of Engineers had placed there to prevent shore erosion.

My friend, Tom Taylor, after observing my plight, took off in his car for home, some two miles away, after advising me that he was going for his pontoon boat to rescue me and tow me to safety. In less than twenty minutes he arrived on the scene with his boat.

However, those twenty minutes were quite "hairy" as the wind and the waves brought me in close proximity to the huge rocks. Fortunately, I was able to use the paddle to fend the boat off from the rocks so that except for some minor scrapes and scratches, the boat was not severely damaged. As soon as Tom threw me a line, the pontoon boat hauled me toward my cove and shortly thereafter, we were in calm, sheltered water where I was able to moor the boat securely.

Retrospective analysis of the situation indicated what a stupid landlubber I was! If I had "dropped the centerboard," the boat would not have drifted sideways and my paddling would have moved me out of danger. Also, if I had opened the air vent screw on the top of the motor gas tank—the motor would have purred like a kitten and taken me to safety.

"Too soon you get old; too late you get smart!"

Thanks to my friend Tom, a potential disaster was averted on my "solo boating venture"! Also, even though I'm somewhat of a "slow learner"—I've never made these same goofs again!

A Matter of Enunciation, Pronunciation, or Accent

After we had lived for a year in our South Carolina home, it became obvious that there was need for some type of outbuilding to house the lawn mowers, roto spader, and other garden and yard equipment. So a decision was made to build one "from scratch" that would complement the construction of the house and yet be adequate for our needs.

With the plans drawn and the construction materials purchased and delivered, I gathered up my tools and began to measure out the selected area and drive stakes into the corner locations. Shortly after I started, our neighbor's son appeared on the scene and after eyeing my tools and the assorted construction materials, he inquired as to what I was "a-goonna make." I told him that I was going to build an outhouse. Since this term didn't register with him, his next inquiry was as to whether he could help me build this. I thanked him but declined his assistance and suggested that he go home and tell his mother that "she wanted him."

He left with a puzzled look on his face but returned some time later with his father. The father, evidently thinking that his son had not understood me, questioned me about "building an outhouse"—since he had noted the construction of our house and knew that there were two bathrooms included in the floor plans. I modified my remark about "outhouse" to "outbuilding" and explained my needs for storage of my yard and garden equipment.

My construction work went along quite rapidly and within a reasonable time period, I proudly completed my new exterior building. The siding and the roof shingles matched those on our home but the structure needed a "finishing touch." My wife, Mary, suggested that perhaps a weathervane might add the right note and volunteered to finance the cost of a weathervane for the new structure. After looking through catalogs and visiting several stores, the choice of a weathervane (at the volunteered price) came down to four different ones:

1. a rooster or gamecock (the mascot of the University of South Carolina);

2. a bulldog (the mascot of the University of Georgia, where our younger daughter had graduated);

3. a tiger (the mascot of Clemson University, which is located only some fifteen miles away);

4. a horse (which would be symbolic of the horsepower contained in the various machines and yet let me avoid any controversy concerning favoritism for any one institution of higher learning).

I chose the horse and we dedicated the building after I installed the weather vane as our Horse House! Some of our well-meaning friends, however, tended to imply other uses for this building and by deliberate mispronunciation, slurred enunciation, or accented innuendo caused us some embarrassment locally. My sister-in-law, Joan, even gave me a cat hat to wear when I went down to supervise operations in my Horse House.

Unfortunately, at about this same time my wife decided to put curtains on the three window areas in our garage door, and since we had some old curtains left from our home in Pennsylvania, decided to use those red curtains. Within days, a neighbor stopped to talk with us on behalf of the next-door church deacons who had evidently heard some of the implications of my construction and in view of the red curtains, seemed to be concerned that we were really planning to open "a house of ill repute" right next to the church!

It took some real convincing before the neighborhood finally accepted my explanation! We even went out and spent the money for new beige curtains and totally rejected all and sundry offers of exterior red lanterns or flood lights to feature our Horse House!

Yes—life can become complicated, even though you have nothing but the best of intentions!

A Sad, Sad Groundhog Day!

On Groundhog Day, 1982, we had the makings of a minor tragedy. Mary stepped out on the garage steps to water an azalea bush beside the house and slipped on the wet top step and fell, severely breaking her right ankle. Since she could not call her plight to my attention readily, it was some time before she was discovered and the neighborhood alerted to arrange for her transportation to the emergency room at the local hospital.

The X rays confirmed the severity of the break and she was scheduled for corrective surgery on the following day (metal pins and screws to hold bones in place). There was obvious intense pain and suffering throughout the night and in the days that followed, even when the ankle and lower leg had been encased in a cast. This first cast was on for about six weeks and the one that followed remained on until April 8. Thus, Mary was either totally or partially immobilized, either in bed or severely inhibited from most activities for about ten weeks.

Flowers, cards, visits, and telephone calls from friends helped somewhat but the discouragement of the continuing confinement was really getting her down until her sister Joan sent her a wall plaque with the following printed on it: GRANT ME PATIENCE, LORD, BUT HURRY!

This plaque was hung on the wall facing her bed, and each morning it became a ritual to repeat this saying *with emphasis* and to repeat it again as she learned to struggle down the hall with her walker and settle down to another day of boredom and confinement.

Perhaps some of her impatience can be attributed to my sincere but somewhat futile efforts at handling the normal household operations of cooking, cleaning, bed making, washing clothes, and so on. I have detailed some of these efforts under separate headings, since perhaps there is an uninitiated person somewhere out there who could benefit from my experiences.

Gourmet Cooking for an Invalid

Since my cooking during our years of marital bliss had been mostly confined to outdoor grilling—steaks, chops, hamburgers, chicken and rotisserie lamb, beef or pork roasts—it was a truly new experience for me to attempt to prepare cuisine that would tempt the palate of someone who "just wasn't hungry." Using three timers, I prepared a variety of meals that really required coordination if every item was to arrive as scheduled—not "mushy," not semi-raw, not salty, not bland—but "just right"! I even learned to use the double-boiler to keep the temperature of the crabmeat stable while the butter sauce was being heated to the correct temperature. Baked potatoes, mashed potatoes, various vegetables with varied cheese sauces or juices I was able to handle. I just didn't fool around with dessert!

Cleaning and Dusting

Because I had been exposed to both a vacuum cleaner and a dust cloth prior to this situation, my only problem here was to spend as much time as possible with Mary and minimize my efforts. Hence, I developed a new technique for vacuuming which I termed "straight-line vacuuming," covering only the cleaning of traffic patterns rather than the movement of furniture, and then developed "swish-and-fluff" dusting which removed surface dust without moving items on tables or cabinets. (I always did have a problem in getting items back where Mary really wanted them.)

Bed Making and Pillow Plumping

Having assisted with bed making over the years, my only problem here was to figure out how the facing on the top sheet went so that it folded back properly. With the area of "pillow plumping," I really got involved with research as to the origin of the expression. According to the research data that I encountered, this expression seems to have originated in the South during the War of The Rebellion, as the ladies of the Atlanta area came into the hospitals to care for the Southern soldiers. Due to the lack of laudanum or other pain-killing drugs, the ladies were helpless to alleviate the pain and suffering of these hospitalized soldiers, so they developed a technique of "plumping their pillows three times with the flat of their hands" and smiled at them and said, "Bless you!"

Anyway, I learned to become an expert "pillow plumper"!

Clothes Washing and Drying

Although this was a new experience, after verbal instruction from Mary and perusal of the washer manual, I managed to get the various items of clothing washed. The drying was a different matter, since I chose to hang them outside on the line. Sounds rather simple doesn't it—until you realize the various rules that accompany something as simple as hanging clothes on the line. In this area, all men's underwear, pajamas, shorts and pants must be hung on the line furthest from a neighbor's house (especially if there is an unmarried female in the house) with the fly-opening toward the west. (We do live in the belt of the prevailing westerlies.) All clothing items must be pre-sorted into proper catergories so that similar items are hung together. Ladies' panties, bras and undergarments should be hung on the middle line so that they will be shielded from view by sheets and pillow cases. Whenever possible, the clothespins should be color coordinated with the various items of clothing (since I'm color blind, this was a real problem to me until I stopped in town and purchased four dozen white clothespins and "went white"). Mary was gentle with me. After viewing clothing on the line, she only inquired, when I made the mistake of hanging up my t-shirts by the shoulders, "Did you hang then that way so there would be room for your angel wings to come through?

Originally, as I planned to write this, I envisioned calling it Blowing in the Wind and relating the story of our life in Pennsylvania, where we had a neighbor (male) who came over to visit us every washday and after wandering through the clothesline area would come into the house for coffee and always ask the same question, "Mary, just what do you put into those *40 D bras* that are out on the line?" Actually, it got so embarrassing that she hung them on a special line down in the laundry room area after some of these remarks.

Pixie Service

In case you wonder, this was my terminology for twenty-four hour, unsolicited service of food, drinks, or "whatever" so that Mary was never wanting for anything—except patience!

Eventually, after serving a three-month internship, I was awarded a special certificate as a House Husband!

CERTIFICATE

Whereas, the trainee has satisfactorily completed an intensive three-month internship program in the various facets of House Husbandry: food purchasing, preparation and serving; superficial cleaning and "swish-and-fluff" dusting; bed making and "pillow plumping"; clothes washing, drying and folding; dish washing and kitchen clean-up; care for personal needs; all correspondence and financial transactions; and, moreover, demonstrated superior competency in "T.L.C." and "pixie service."

This certificate is hereby awarded to

Edward L. Fandt

as a

HOUSE HUSBAND

Given This 11th Day of May, 1982.

Attest: Mary B. Fandt, Supervisor
Internship Training Program

A Unique Wedding Present

When one of our three favorite New Jersey nieces invited us to her wedding in April, 1982, it posed a distinct problem to us, since due to Mary's leg cast, we just could not make the trip. Also, we were in a quandary as to something that would be appropriate for an avowed Civil War buff and a *Gone with the Wind* fanatic. What was there that would conform to the ante-bellum Southern living theme and still remain within the realm of reason and sanity?

As I pondered the problem while riding back and forth

on the mower across our half-acre back lawn, dodging the numerous sweet gum tree burrs in the yard—I developed an idea and, as it evolved, approached Mary with it as a suggestion for a gift. She reluctantly agreed to look at the finished product before granting a final approval.

The project was initiated: I collected a dozen sweet gum tree burrs (approximately two inches in diameter with porcupinelike spines on the outside); sprayed these burrs with spray paint (I had eight different colors in my workshop area); constructed a nine-compartment, egg-type cardboard box and lined the three-inch spaces with cotton; typed up a set of directions and an accompanying letter; and packaged the product for Mary's review and possible approval before shipment.

Dear Betsy,

Knowing of your deep interest in the ante-bellum South, we have been challenged to find an appropriate wedding gift that would encompass this theme.

I have, purportedly, consulted with an ancient colored mammy and posed the question to her, "How did y'all prepare your Southern young ladies for marriage? Was it something that you told them or was there some type of training program that they went through to help them?"

Her answer was most direct. "Properly brung-up young ladies *never* was allowed to talk about sex or marital relations, but they was given a bridal kit to help them in handling the situation!"

She then proceeded to give me general directions which I have attempted to follow in constructing the attached kit.

Please understand our underlying purpose in sending this to you. Since we do not know whether or not your husband has a real sense of humor, perhaps it will not be appropriate to share it with him. In that case, just share with him the U.S. Savings Bonds which are being sent under separate cover!

Love,
Aunt Mary and Uncle Ed

BETSY'S BRIDAL KIT

(Interior card) These are color-coded, dehydrated

Porcupine Eggs

They will continue in their dormant state
unless subjected to continued human body heat.

(Interior card)

Directions

1. Leave a light on in the bedroom.
2. Place the appropriate "egg/eggs" (see code below) in the middle of the conjugal bed—more toward *his* side.
3. Simulate sleep!

Color Code Meanings

Black .... Too late!
Green .... Stomachache!
Brown .... Backache!
Gold .... Pregnant!
White .... Too tired!
Blue .... Head ache!
Yellow .... *Not* tonight!
Red .... Monthly period!★
★(*Eight* colors—extra Red)

No "egg/eggs" . . . . ready, willing, available!

In case the light is extinguished, or the groom is color blind, do not worry—he'll "get the point"!

The letter, directions and the kit were sent via U.P.S. to Betsy at her mother's house with a note to her mother to have Betsy open them *only* when she was alone.

The day of the wedding arrived and we waited, with some fear and trepidation, to hear from the family as to the progress of events. That evening we had a telephone call from Betsy from her mother's house where the close family friends had gathered after the reception. She was hilarious over her bridal kit and had shown it to most of the wedding party, with the exception of her new mother-in-law, and it was considered to be the "most unique wedding gift" that had ever been devised!

P.S. They also appreciated the bonds!

The Local Minister Came To Visit

During the summer after my wife's recovery from her broken ankle, we had a visit from the new minister of the local church next to our home. I had just finished mowing the lawn and after taking a shower and donning my pajamas, was relaxing on the back porch when I heard this male voice inside the house talking to Mary and her sister Joan. I entered just in time to hear his explanation that although he knew we did not belong to the church, he had heard that Mary had been incapaciated for some time and, that since none of his local parishioners were at home, he and his wife just wanted to stop in to say "Hello."

After checking to make sure that I was "decent," I barged in and, with apologies for my pajama ensemble, did manage to get engaged in the conversation. The five of us had a delightful conversation during which I proudly displayed my House Husband Certificate (which I had just recently awarded myself) and explained to him some of the terminology used in the certificate—"swish-and-fluff dusting," "pillow-plumping" (and its origin in the South during the Civil War), "round-the-clock Pixie Service," and so on.

After an hour or so, he suggested leaving and, since we were of a different religion, asked if it would be acceptable if he said a prayer before he left.

I replied, "Reverend, go ahead with the prayer—just as long as you don't take up a collection afterward!"

He acknowledged my request, led us in prayer, and then he and his wife departed.

I was rather soundly berated after they left for "my flip tongue" and irreverent manner and was consigned to the "dog house" for penitential reflections.

About a year later, following an operation that Mary had undergone, the minister and his wife again came to call upon us to wish her a speedy recovery and to visit with us. Remembering that I had been "rude" to him on his previous visit, I apoligized for my remarks about the collection. It didn't bother him in the least, he explained. "Hence, today, he would ask his wife to take up a silent collection!"

Another nice visit—good conversation, meaningful prayers—another vignette in our Southern life-style!

A Strange Visitor during the Ides of March

While we were waiting for the arrival of the mailman, which is really the big event of the day in our somewhat dull and prosaic life, Mary saw a strange animal in our front yard and called my attention to it. I looked, and after some discussion we concurred that it was a large horned goat. It was trailing a broken rope from its neck so evidently it was a domesticated animal.

Although I had been awarded the honor of catching the goat, the animal had not been advised of this and was not receptive to my efforts to retrieve the rope. Every time I managed to get fairly close, the goat began bleating at me with a high-pitched "Na-a-a-a-a-a" sound and moved out of my grasping range. Frustrated after several attempts, I replied with a deeper-toned "Na-a-a-a-a" of my own and edged closer. No luck! Finally the goat trotted off through the cemetery and into the woods.

About a half-hour later, the goat returned and stared at us through our front bay window and bleated at us again. I finally accepted the challenge and went outside in an effort to capture the creature. After numerous exchanges of "bleats" between us, I still was unable to grasp the trailing rope and gave up the effort and went into the garage to work, leaving the garage side door open—just in case the goat became lonesome. To my surprise, some ten minutes later the goat wandered in through the open doorway and as we exchanged "bleats," followed me as I slowly walked around our car. Although I still couldn't get close enough to grab the trailing rope, I finally manuevered all the way around the car and closed the outside door!

Captured! Now what to do with it? Since it had been Mary's idea that I catch the goat, I asked her to call Mike Taylor at the nearby local store to determine whether he might know of anyone in the area who had lost a goat. Fortunately he did and was able to locate the owner who promised to come for the goat shortly.

In the meantime, the goat seemed to be hungry—but spurning the offer of a slice of bread, began to eat (1) a paper bag, (2) the plastic covering of the new door sitting in the garage, (3) my work shoes, (4) slivers of loose plywood on the interior of the garage door, (5) the branches from a dead gardenia plant—at the same time continually emitting "Na-a-a-a-a-a's."

I finally was able to grasp the trailing rope which was fastened around the goat's neck, but because of her size and determination, we only moved in the direction that she wanted to go. Eventually, she even allowed me to pet her and scratch her head in the area between her rather large horns. Although it seemed obvious from her distended bag that she needed to be milked, I decided that since my hands were cold, it might be safer for both me and our car if I passed up this opportunity to display my skills. No butts wanted!

Eventually, the owner arrived, thanked us—and took off with the goat, sadly bleating at me from the back of the truck as they left!

Several days later, after relating the story to several of our friends, even including my version of the "Na-a-a-a-a's," I decided that April 1 would be an appropriate day to award myself the attached citation from a non-existent organization—signed by a fictitious person I remembered from my youth at the county fairs, as her name was frequently announced over the loudspeakers to those persons who had lost a purse, clothing, or other items, Go to Helen Hunt for the missing articles!

The Toggenburg Capricorn Society, N. E.

SPECIAL CITATION AND AWARD

Whereas, on March 21, 1983, the recipient of this special commendation did at great risk to his personal safety and health, and by the utilization of superior acumen and true compassion, plus demonstrated proficiency in the imitation of the mating call of the Toggenburg doe—did entice and rescue from the wild boondocks of Starr, South Carolina, a mature, distraught, strayed Toggenburg female goat, and having captured said animal, was sucessful in reuniting said animal with her legitimate owner.

Therefore, since such actions are deemed to be worthy of note, it is with great pride that the Society does award and proclaim the title of

Honorary Goat Apprehender

to

Edward L. Fandt

Given on April 1, 1983 at Starr, South Carolina.

Attest: Helen Hunt, Coordinator
          Lost and Strayed Division
          Toggenburg Capricorn Society

Suspended Citizenship

When Yankees move to South Carolina, they normally go through a four-year probationary period before they are recognized as South Carolinians.

During this time period, they are carefully observed as to their compliance with certain unwritten rules and regulations:

1. Do they say "Y'all!" instead of "You-all!"?

2. Do they wave to local cars that they meet on two-lane highways?

3. In paying for goods or store-bought items, do they generally use "old" one-, five-, and ten-dollar bills, instead of flaunting "new" twenty-dollar bills?

4. Do they refrain from using the following terms in their reference to local residents: "Red Necks," "Local Yokels," "Georgia Crackers," "Good Old Boys"?

5. Do they observe Generals Robert E. Lee and Stonewall Jackson's birthdays with proper reverence?

6. When they discuss their local taxes—instead of giving exact amounts or bragging how low taxes really are, do they only complain about the percentage of increase over the previous year (Ex., sales tax went up by twenty-five percent—from four cents to five cents; county tax on property went up fifty percent—from $90 to $135)?

7. In local restaurants, do they accept "grits" and "hush puppies" on their plates without loudly complaining that they "Jest kaint stan' em"?

Mary and I faithfully followed these seven basic rules for three years and eleven months—and then, *disaster struck!*

During May, 1983, our roses were blooming prolifically so we decided to pick a spare dozen and share them with a wonderful native South Carolina couple who had been so kind and friendly to us and who had showered us with their garden produce for the past three years. Unfortunately, the roses that we picked and gave to them were of a variety known as Mr. Lincoln,—hence, with the memories of the Civil War and Abraham Lincoln still fresh in the minds of local residents, this gift was construed to be a deep insult!

Accordingly, Mary and I have been informally advised that we must now serve as additional three years of probationary behavior before the suspension of our South Carolina citizenship will even be reconsidered!

"The road to hell is paved with good intentions"—but at least most of our ex-Yankee neighbors continued speaking to us and the storekeepers still accepted our "long green" funds that we had brought South with us!

Where, Oh Where Did I Put the Anchor?

I had encountered a problem with the anchor on my sailboat dragging during heavy western winds on the lake, even when I supplemented the weight of the anchor with one or more cement blocks.

During the drought of 1983, I finally had a chance to remedy the situation. The lake level was down some eighteen feet so I walked out about twenty-five feet from the shore on our side of the cove and dug a hole for a permanent anchor installation. This home-made anchor consisted of two circular cement slabs thirty inches in diameter with a two-foot–square slab in between (all slabs were two inches thick) and bolted together with a ten-inch ring bolt equipped with a swivel ring on the top; total weight, some seventy pounds.

After carefully burying this anchor in the thick clay so that only the swivel ring was exposed, I proceeded to chart the exact location. "From a dead pine tree stump on our side of the cove, twenty paces NNW from the shoreline in line with a large pine tree on the point corner of the cove on the opposite shore" were my recorded directions.

However, when the boat went into the water next May, I couldn't find the anchor! Carefully consulting my chart, I sighted across the cove to the pine tree on the opposite side— but the pine tree was no longer there! During the spring storms, obviously, the tree had blown down and the point of land where it had been located was totally eroded. Also, the shoreline on our side of the cove had eroded several feet in places—so my recorded "twenty paces NNW" left a rather large under- water area to search.

When our younger daughter visited us for a few days, I elicited her help in locating the anchor. We probed the cove bottom with rakes and a shovel in the approximate area and then began diving and swimming underwater in the six-foot depth, carefully searching the bottom for either signs of the metal swivel or the top of the concrete slab but found nothing but mud and clay!

Some time later I related my plight to a retired lake-ranger friend but didn't get too much sympathy from him—just a story from his lake experiences which tended to point out my stupidity.

"Two city fellers came out to go fishin' on the lake. They rented a boat, loaded their rods and gear aboard and went a-fishin'. At the end of the day they returned without having caught a single fish. The next day they came back again and still no luck! They tried again on the third day. This time, after about an hour, the fish really began biting and by noon they had caught their quota. One of the fishermen called out to the t'other un to mark the place so that they could come back again to the same spot. Grabbing a scaling knife, he began cutting a notch in the bow of the boat—then stopped and asked, 'Supposin' we don't git this same boat?' Yep, they were real city fellers!"

Then the ex-ranger proceeded to explain that the Army Corps of Engineers does not allow permanent anchors in the lake except by special permits, usually issued only to marinas. Thus, by losing my anchor, I had really saved myself from a substantial fine. All is well that ends well!

Not Guilty, as Almost Charged!

During a visit to us during the summer of 1983, our daughter Patty insisted on cleaning, waxing and refurbishing our sailboat (the one that she formerly owned) and getting it into the water in operational condition. After three days of labor in ninety-degree temperatures, the boat was scrubbed, rinsed and waxed (mostly by Patty) and after new replacement lines were added as needed, was ready for launching into Hartwell Lake. In the cleansing process, the registration numbers SC 661 were removed from both sides of the bow. At the time this did not seem to be a problem since I had purchased replacement instant-stick letters and numbers and planned to install them before using the boat.

No problem until I waded out in armpit-depth water two days later to stick them in place. Due to the semi-crippled condition of my right hand and a ten knot lake wind, some of the letters and numbers were slightly wavy. Having finished one side semi-satisfactorily, I was applying the final "S" to the other side—when a fish bit me! The "S" went on sideways and since it was instant-stick, I just couldn't manage to position it properly. Of course, this was just the moment for the Marine Patrol boat to put in an appearance and evalute the situation! (At the time, South Carolina was conducting dual campaigns against driving under the influence and illiteracy, and all law enforcement officers had been alerted to strictly enforce the laws.)

The two patrolmen in the boat, after carefully looking over my lettering efforts, began to question me and advised me that they were considering charging me with either or both "Lettering Under the Influence" and "Illiteracy."

Obviously, I protested and cited the Carter Episode Plea (remember when President Jimmy Carter was attacked on the water by a giant killer rabbit) and contended that I had been subjected to "disconcertation due to a piscatorial assault" (I didn't bother to explain that the fish was only some five inches long!). Since it seemed doubtful to me that either of the patrolmen understood just what I meant since I was asked to repeat it several times and then even spelled it correctly (they guessed!). I further explained that the apparent waviness of the letters and numbers was due to the waves on the lake and *not* because I was under the influence. After all, it was early morning and it is a known fact that I never (almost never) have a drink until the sun is over the yardarm, somewhere after 11:00 A.M.

Furthermore, I was planning on submitting the sideway "S" to the South Carolina Marine Resources Department as an experimental symbol for use on boats that are owned or operated by Handicapped Senior Citizens.

After considerable head-scratching, the officers left without issuing a summons to me—probably wondering why they had the misfortune to encounter such a character on a pleasant day on beautiful Hartwell Lake!

25

Under Attack!

We were awakened at 6:00 A.M. on April 11, 1984, by a "rat-ta-tat-rat-ta-tat" sound. Our first thoughts were to check the TV to ascertain whether it was a late-late show repeat of either *Desert Rats* or *The A Team*. It wasn't the TV, so it must be something outside tapping on the house. Shortly thereafter, there was a metallic rat-ta-tat sound in the area of the back gutter. We dismissed it as an early bird pecking at seeds in the gutter (later it became apparent that the little dear was really in the process of sharpening its beak).

The situation was repeated every morning for the next week. Our only relief from the early-morning disturbance occurred when one of us went out on the back deck near our bedroom area and banged on the gutter with either our hand or a magazine. Then it stopped for ten or fifteen minutes before starting in again in a different location.

During the following week, after stealthful surveillance of the western end of our house, we detected a bird, clinging to the weather board near to the roof, pecking away with its beak at the weatherboard and making the very rat-ta-tat-rat-ta-tat sound that had awakened us on prior occasions.

Since we were unable to supply a clear description of the bird to the South Carolina Ornithology Society (who sees clearly at 6:00 A.M. and is able to describe a flying bird, especially if the observer is color blind?) it was strictly a suggestion that due to the heavy winds in the area that had recently blown down numerous dead trees, possibly it was an introverted South Carolina woodpecker (*Dendrocopos villosus*) that had lost its favorite tree and had now selected our house as the "target of its efforts."

Further early-morning obsevations and a ladder-climbing inspection confirmed the identity of the bird and the fact that it had pecked through the weatherboard in four separate areas with holes that ranged in size from a silver dollar to a quarter. Also, several of the other siding boards and corner boards were splintered in places where the attack had been concentrated.

Consultation with the S.C.O.S., with neighbors and some of our friends provided us with varied remedial suggestions:

1. "Shoot the bird"—however, with my aim (if we had a gun), this would probably result in more holes in the house than the bird had made. Also, since this is a protected bird, it is illegal to shoot it. *Not a practical answer!*

2. "Spray the exterior wood surface with a poison spray"— however, since we still had to live in the house and it would be illegal to poison the bird—*this was rejected!*

3. "Paint the weatherboard a deep purple color since this bird has a known aversion to this color." We seriously considered this but because it would look like HELL next to the church on this side of the house, *this was rejected!*

4. "Attach strips of fluttering white cloth to the edge of the roof as a deterrent to the bird." After trying this, all we had was the appreciation of the local nesting birds who promptly removed the strips of cloth and used them in their nest construction. A *waste of time and effort!*

5. "Hang a scarecrow or human effigy on the peak of the house to scare the bird away." This is prohibited by the local cemetery regulations, except during Halloween; hence, *This was considered impractical!*

6. "Nail copper sheathing strips over the wood and paint them a brown color so that the bird would break its beak when it pecked away at the wood." *Plausible but expensive!*

7. "Hire a mason and have this end of the house bricked up and a concrete cornice installed in place of the weatherboard." *Expensive and time-consuming, but possible!*

8. "Plug the holes with wood filler. Mix a quarter-pound of gum arabic and two ounces of powdered glue in a quart of exterior latex brown paint and apply as a first coat over the

wood; add six tablespoons of Kaopectate Concentrate and two ounces each of alum and natural resin to the paint, mix thoroughly, and apply liberally as a second coat." This local formula, known as P.B.E. (plugging both ends), should inhibit the bird from further pecking after several good bites! *Our current solution! Time alone would tell whether or not it worked!*

We enjoyed five days of peace and quiet! On May 6, obviously "purged" of the edibles that we had supplied, the bird attacked with renewed vim and vigor. Avoiding the weatherboard, it randomly attacked wooden areas with furious efforts and, when the rains came, shifted to the front of the house where the three-foot overhang gave it protection from the weather.

A frantic telephone call to the local county agricultural agent elicited the following, after a detailed description of our problem: 'The woodpecker had evidently staked out our house as his territory and there was, from their experience with over one hundred similar cases, only one known way to solve the problem. Using a .410 gauge shotgun, loaded with light bird shot— SHOOT THE BIRD!"

Action on this was deferred because we were leaving in the near future on a scheduled trip to Texas. Upon our return, if the house was still standing, we would finalize arrangements to borrow a gun, construct a "blind or shelter" and begin waiting for the dear bird every morning with the fervent hope that I'll be able to "wing him" and leave the house still intact.

There is one positive factor to consider—since the bird will not be on daylight saving time, I won't have to begin my vigil in the blind until an hour later, having managed an hour in my favor with the time change!

An Update on the "Under Attack" Story

When we returned from our ten-day trip to Texas, it was obvious that our woodpecker friend had really enjoyed our absence.

The weatherboards (facia boards) near the roof on both ends of the house had been attacked again (several more half-dollar sized holes pecked through); the rough-saw cedar boards at the four corners of the house and around the windows were splintered and contained numerous peck-holes; the main cedar support posts and the siding on both ends and the front of the house were riddled with innumerable new holes.

The decision was made: "SHOOT THE BIRD!"

Then I encountered both red tape and some vigorous protests!

Red Tape

1. When I attempted to apply for a fee exemption on a special hunting license, I was advised that (a) I must produce a copy of a recent regular hunting license issued to me (a problem since I've never had one! Back in my youthful days *before* I met my wife, admittedly I did hunt dears and bares— but no license was necessary!); or (b) demonstrate that I had proficiency in handling firearms (my marksman medal for machine gun issued to me at C.M.T.C. in 1934 was not considered acceptable); and (c) produce attested certification as to the specific bird and a written estimate of the damage incurred from this bird.

2. To obtain a special building permit to construct two temporary bird blinds at either end of the house— I must submit, in triplicate, detailed sketches of the blinds, including the sizes of the various wood pieces to be used and the tensil strength of the fiberglass roofing; the exact locations of the blinds; the estimated cost, including labor, of the blinds; and the specific time duration that the blinds would be on the site.

3. Also, a surety bond must be posted with the local power company to cover any and all costs, including disruption of service, in case any of the local wires, cables or transformers should be damaged by stray shots. Thank goodness that all of the area telephone service is underground so a second surety bond was not necessary!

Protests

1. My two daughters were shocked that their father, who had brought them up to love and care for all animals and birds, would consider such action!

2. A bird-watcher friend from New Jersey wrote to me vehementaly protesting that "I should *not* shoot the bird."

3. A friend from Florida, well-versed in bird lore, wrote and suggested that when the woodpecker located a mate, the attacks would undoubtedly cease. "Have patience!"

4. My dear wife—aware of my total lack of knowledge concerning guns and, perhaps, fearful of her safety—did not really protest. She "suggested" that there has to be another solution!

As a Result . . .

We hired a siding contractor to replce the damaged areas at both ends of the house and then cover the existing siding with heavy-duty vinyl siding and the facia boards and the cedar window, door and corner framings with matching heavy-duty aluminum boxing.

In the meantime, at the suggestion of a retired forest ranger, I constructed a twelve-inch wooden owl, painted it gray with a few touches of black; attached a vicious-looking yellow beak and two reflective eyes (one red—stop pecking at our house!; one green—go away to some other place!) and stapled two fluttering yellow ribbons to its feet. This grotesque object was then hung at the front of the house in the heaviest woodpecker attack area.

As additional measures, we fastened an eight-inch white ceramic cat with fluttering red ribbons tied to its tail some eight feet up on the main cedar post in the front of the house and placed a large black iron cat with a yellow bow around its neck and fluttering white and purple ribbons tied to its tail in the front of the house near the garage area.

The woodpecker never appeared again! The siding contractor completed his repairs and installations without interruption.

THIS IS THE END OF THE WOODPECKER TALE!

An Informal Hearing

BEFORE: The Honorable Travis D. Uffjustis, Esq.
Plenipotentiary Judge The Thirteenth Out-and-Around Court
Anderson County, South Carolina

PLAINTIFFS: Edward L. Fandt and Mary B. Fandt, represented by Ms. I. Emma Chyster, Attorney-at-Law

SUBJECT: Whereas, the above-listed plaintiffs do state and affirm that on the thirty-second day of April, 1983, they were capriciously, summarily and *de summa non causa* deprived of their South Carolina citizenship for an inadvertent gift of a bouquet of Mr. Lincoln roses to a native South Carolina couple, and

Whereas, the plaintiffs contend and asseverate that the three-year probationary period before reconsideration of the subject is acrimonious, has imposed undue hardship and has negatively inhibited their social and business activities, and

Whereas, the probationary edit has deeply and inversely impinged upon the true character and friendly nature of the plaintiffs,

Therefore, the plaintiffs do petition that the probationary edict be expunged from their records and that total amelioration be granted, together with complete South Carolina Citizenship.

EVIDENCE: The attorney for the plaintiffs presented both documentary and verbal testamentary data to the effect that:

1. The above-mentioned male plaintiff is legally color blind.

2. The rose bush from which the alleged Mr. Lincoln roses were picked is incorrectly tagged and labeled since it actually produces pink, not red roses.

3. The plaintiffs have demonstrated over the past four years a deep, communicative rapport with their nearest neighbors (the occupants of the Ruhamah Church Cemetery).

32

RULING: The plaintiffs, Edward L. Fandt and Mary B. Fandt, shall be granted full citizenship in South Carolina as of the conclusion of their five-year residency period, effective on June 16, 1984.

DATED: June 1, 1984
ATTESTED: Travis D. Uffjustis, Judge

Hear Ye! Hear Ye! Hear Y'all!

"As time goes by," it's a known fact that engines, appliances and even the human body tend to slow down or perform at less-then-optimum levels. My dear wife, Mary, after some five years of deteriorating hearing acuity, finally conceded this fact when, with the TV speakers vibrating at the maximum sound level, she admitted that she just "could not understand the conversation."

Accordingly, she visited an otolaryngologist who, after an examination and hearing tests, advised her that her hearing was at the forty to fifty percent level. Since this was not an operable condition, he recommended that she consider a hearing aid as a supplement to her hearing.

We next visited an audiologist who confirmed the previous diagnosis and measured her for a hearing aid. After the aid arrived some two weeks later, she was instructed in the operation, care and insertion of the aid.

The following day we left on a trip to Nashville to visit the Grand Ole Opry. The aid seemed to work quite well on the trip—although there were some complaints about how loud my voice was, how noisy the air conditioner sounded, the roar of the car engine—all sounds that she had not heard clearly for years!

All went well until we sat down in the Opry House in our front-row seats in the center section only some eight feet away from the performers. Then as the program began and the amplifiers blasted—Mary actually jumped about eighteen inches into the air before she could "tone-down" her hearing aid.

Over subsequent weeks, she learned to live with it and make the necessary adjustments to varying situations. As she says, "It's not the same as my natural hearing but it does help." She still has trouble with group cross-talk, loud noises, and children's screams, and great difficulty when people talk "southernese" to her.

My point in writing this article is not to embarrass my wife because of her hearing impairment but to laud her for her positive attitude and perseverance in coping with the situation.

Perhaps if I finally complete the six-week therapy program that the audiologist recommended for me to tone down the decible quality of my voice, this will be helpful to her. Also, I have promised her that when it becomes necessary to replace the current hearing aid (which was manufactured in Minnesota), we will procure one that is manufactured in the South where "southernese" is spoken!

Our Trip to Music City, U.S.A.

Each year since we have been in South Carolina, my wife's sister Joan usually spends two weeks of her vacation with us. We have done some wandering, even as far as Texas, but in

1984 we decided to remain somewhat within easy driving range. Accordingly, even though none of the three of us are country western music lovers, the decision was to visit the Grand Ole Opry in Nashville, Tennessee. Since we had been advised that tickets should be ordered well in advance, we wrote in February and sent a check for three matinee tickets for August 10, 1984, and a short commentary that since we were senior citizens with some sight and hearing problems, we would appreciate having seats in an area where we could see and hear the performers. The ticket notice was received and we were advised to pick up our tickets on August 10, in the morning.

During the intervening months, we pored over the various press releases from Nashville as to accommodations, visitation areas, entertainment and dining guides. In addition, to get us in the mood for this type of entertainment, my wife and I began to watch the weekly Hee Haw T.V. show to become acclimated to the songs, jokes, costumes and format of this type of program.

We left on our one-day ride to Nashville via Atlanta on August 9 and arrived without incident at our motel in the near vicinity of the Grand Old Opry. The room accommodations were satisfactory, except for the ice machine that was not operational. I ended up going to the lounge for ice until my wife met the buxom barmaid on our way to dinner, thence, my wife "volunteered" to replenish the ice as needed.

I picked up our tickets the next morning and was really surprised to discover that the three tickets were in the exact center of the first row, just some eight feet from the performers. Super Seats!

The two-and-one-half-hour program was superb!—just hand-clapping, foot-stomping music in a total atmosphere of friendliness and companionship! (Warning to visitors: since there are no intermissions at the matinee performances, go to the bathroom before you settle down in your seat!)

On the next day we decided to take the two and one-half hour trip on the scenic paddle-wheel cruise boat on the Cumberland River. Again, most enjoyable, due to a superior guide and song-leader who involved the passengers in varied activities and songs!

Trouble reared its ugly head when we returned from the cruise and I discovered a three-dollar parking ticket on our car! When I had parked the car all three of us took note of the numbered space—"33"—and then I placed four quarters (one for each hour) in the numbered parking area box "33." It seems that the parking authority must have used illiterate convict labor to stencil the numbers of the parking areas since I was being fined for parking in area "83," which showed up as "33" since the left half of the stencil had never been painted. Since there was no live person to argue with, I deposited the fine in the correct container and left, "muttering to myself"!

We wandered in the downtown Music City, U.S.A. area for several hours, visiting the Country Music Hall of Fame and Museum, Ryman Auditorium, Music Row, the Country Music Wax Museum and Mall, plus other assorted tourist traps. I later wrote postcards to several of our friends about this phase of our visit, indicating that I managed to stand next to Dolly Parton, about sixteen inches from her! In a subsequent card, I really did explain that my proximity to Dolly was only in the wax museum exhibit.

After a delicious dinner, we planned for our next venture on Sunday—a visit to Andrew Jackson's home, The Hermitage. Another delightful day without pressure as we wandered through the gardens, the museum and the actual home of Rachel and Andrew Jackson.

I was almost ready to spend an additional visitation day in the area until, as we stopped for gasoline, one of my credit cards "cracked in half." This seemed to me to be a gentle hint that it was time for us to head for home.

In spite of the female protestations, we set out for South

Carolina on Monday morning, following a different route that would take us through the Great Smokies and into Asheville and Greenville. It was on this section of the trip that there developed a divergence of opinion.

As we were traveling up and down the hills of the Great Smokies, we tended to play games with a truck that first passed us—and then we passed, as we climbed up the hills. As it passed us, there was a flurry of chicken feathers flying through the air; as we passed it on the up-hill stretch, the driver seemed to be leaning out of the cab and beating on the sides of the chicken crates with a bamboo garden rake.

After some time we finally stopped at a rest stop for relief and this is where our divergence of opinion really developed. Mary and Joan went to the ladies' room while I stayed with our vehicle. I discovered that the "chicken truck" was parked nearby so I ventured over to talk with the driver, asking him just what the meaning of the bamboo rake and the beating on the side of the truck had to do with his operation.

"My boss had a breakdown of another truck this morning and since we must have this load of chickens in Asheville today, he double-loaded me and stated that he had read in a magazine article that if the chickens or at least half of them could be "kept flying," there would be a one-half reduction in the gross weight."

So far, using the technique of beating on the sides of the crates, he had been able to get up the steep hills into North Carolina. However, he was studying the map of the road ahead since there were two weigh stations up the road and he was trying to figure out a bypass of these areas.

We departed after Mary and Joan returned from the rest room area—hence, the divergence of opinion concerning the "chicken truck"! They never did meet the driver.

In spite of some rain and drizzle, we made our return journey through Asheville, Greenville, and Anderson to our home base on Lake Hartwell safely!

A Name Change:
From "Our" House to the Owl House

After my printed release to some twenty of my regular correspondents (My Episode-of-the-Month Club), in which I attributed the disappearance of the pesky woodpecker to the advent of my self-constructed "grotesque owl," we have received several more owls from some of our well-intentioned friends.

A nine-inch brass wind chime owl with six smaller dangling owls; a twelve-inch plastic owl; a carved wooden plaque featuring a hand-painted burrowing owl and the quotation, "I don't give a hooot" (the extra "o" to give it a southern accent); a bake-it-yourself colored glass owl window hanger; and a package of one hundred "owl" return address stickers for the Fandts' correspondence.

A recent inventory of our various owl possessions indicated that in addition to the above-mentioned acquisitions, we have two interior owl mobiles; three outdoor owl wind chimes with bamboo clackers; a welcome doormat with two owls "Welcome to Our Nest"; two twelve-inch ceramic owls with interior tapers for burning; a nine-inch hanging owl with movable eyes, handmade from pine cones; one twelve-inch ceramic owl hanging ashtray, and one six-inch owl-shaped candle.

Please, Friends—No more owls!

In retrospect, things could have been worse! Just suppose that we had attibuted the disappearance of the woodpecker to the presence of the two back-up cats (one white; one black) that I placed outside with the grotesque owl—then we might have had to change the name of Our House to Fandt's Cat House!—or Heaven Forbid, just suppose that we had used the symbol of my fictitious sister, Ella Fandt, and ended up with a herd of elephants in the yard or in the house!

The Mailman Cometh Later!
And Later! And Later!

Perhaps to most people it really doesn't matter—but to retirees, the arrival of the mailman is the big event of the day. The local paper arrives, correspondence from friends is read avidly, and the bills are reviewed and consigned to this month's paper bag (at the end of the month we have a "grab-it session", reaching into the bag to determine which bills we pay until we reach the limit of our checking account and consign the remainder to next month's bag). Then we review the sucker mail—"Send ten dollars for a Real Diamond"; "You have WON A PRIZE—send money to assure your eligibility; "You are eligible for a weekend vacation and fabulous prizes if you will just visit Lake Blah Blah and just listen to a short promotional talk and film extolling the marvelous facilities at this new resort development."

When we first moved to our present location in South Carolina, the mailman regularly arrived at 9:30 A.M., except on Thursdays and the first of each month, when he arrived at 10:00 A.M. Accordingly, we adjusted our life style to this time schedule and leisurely sipped our coffee and awaited his arrival.

Then a new mailman took over some two years ago and forget the time schedule! Now we are fortunate if he even arrives at 11:30 A.M.—and two days a week, his substitute manages to arrive sometime between noon and 1:15 P.M.

How much coffee??? can you drink in the additional two or three hours?

With this disrupted day . . . instead of planning to do yard work or other outdoor activities after reading the paper and having lunch, now I end up thinking about the work and am mentally exhausted even before I actually get-around-to-it in mid-afternoon!

Now that the postal service has announced an increase in postal rates so that the employees can receive a "well-deserved raise," I suppose that we can look forward to late afternoon deliveries—and, perhaps, be advised that we must install a light on our rural mailbox so that the mailman can find it at night!

Batman! Batman! Where Are You?

After my experiences with the woodpecker attack on our house and my solutions to that problem, as reported in the *Country Journal* and various releases to the members of my Episode-of-the-Month Club, I was prepared for requests for my semi-expertise on similar problems.

Recently I received my first request from a friend in New Jersey (the same one who so vehemently wrote to me, "Don't kill the woodpecker!").

It seems that early in January, a bat invaded their house—probably came down the fireplace chimmney in their den, squeezed around the closed damper and then began to fly about in their living room. Since she had just hung new curtains in the living room, they began to chase it frantically around the house and attempted to open the front door and drive it outside. It did not go out the front door but *disappeared!*

Two days later it reappeared and again flew about in the living room area. After more frenzied chasing with a broom, it seemed to get winded and landed on the floor for a few moments. Then it became smaller as it folded up its wings to mouse size and, again disappeared under the furniture. After carefully cleaning the living room and turning over all of the furniture cautiously, my friend Nell wrote to me and asked, "Ed, what would you do?"

A challenging problem! However, since I had just read a most interesting article in *The Country Journal* titled "The Threat of Rabies," dealing with the problem of how bats tend to spread rabies, I immediately continued with further research relevant to the problem and formulated the following suggestions for her consideration:

1. Borrow one of your granddaughter's doll houses and have your husband convert it to a church by adding a steeple out of plywood. Leave an opening in the steeple large enough for the bat to enter and inside, install a mousetrap baited with a mixture of peanut butter and tuna fish. (Remember that bats do have a known affinity for a belfry!)

2. Hang a birdcage in the living room with an open trigger-door that would activate if the bat enters the cage to attack a fake mouse which should be suspended by its tail inside the cage.

3. Borrow a black female cat from a friend or neighbor (be sure that the cat has had rabies shots!) and place its food dish in the living room somewhere near the place where you last saw the bat when it disappeared. Clean up the bat's wings the very next day since the cat will not eat them.

4. Close up the house and go on vacation for at least three weeks. Upon your return, gently pick up the bat's remains with a dustpan. If there is a slight odor, just follow your nose and check under your furniture again!

Remember that this was free advice and you do know what you get for nothing!

Incidentally, be warned that due to inflation, I will be doubling my consultant fee as of April 1!

Shortly thereafter, these friends advised us that the bat had reappeared *before* my suggestions had arrived and with a lucky swipe of a flyswatter, had been knocked to the floor and "crushed underfoot"!

After reviewing my suggestions and sending me a note of thanks for my interest, they decided that item four, "close up the house and go on vacation," was most appealing to them; hence, they embarked on a two-week golfing and visiting trip and vacation!

"Do You Know What a Damifi Is?"

During a recent trip to Texas we had occasion to stop in the lounge of the motel where we were staying in order to take advantage of the two complimentary cocktails that the establishments had offered us. Much to my surprise there was a sign on the bar that asked a question, "Do you know what's in this drink? DAMIFINO!"

This brought back memories of my usage of the term *Damifi* over the years. When the Japanese beetles decimated my wax bean plant leaves, leaving behind only the veined outline of the leaves, I salvaged the remains, sprayed them with gold paint, framed them and sent them to some of my friends with the caption "A GOLDEN DAMIFI" and an explanation "I'll be *damned if I* know why the beetles chose to eat my bean leaves in this manner!" Then later, when I planted a variety of flowering plants and flowers around my fountain pool area and misplaced my chart indicating the names and varieties of the plants, I replied to visitors who inquired as to the name of the plant or flower, "They are yellow (or blue; or pink; or any appropriate color) DAMIFIS!"

When we moved to our present location in South Carolina, our two daughters gave us four green bushes to plant in the front yard as a house-warming present. Since we never did know the correct name for these bushes, whenever visitors admired them and questioned me as to their variety, I simply replied in a straightforward manner, "They are green DAMIFIS."

This past Christmas we were at the Christmas buffet at the Marriott Hotel in Tampa and on one of my trips back from the buffet area, I stopped to admire some of the many live plants that lined the passageway. I was somewhat surprised when a rather mature lady stopped next to me and inquired as to whether I knew what type of plant the one in front of me was. Since she seemed to be quite serious about it, I pondered for a moment before I explained that I believed that it was, "A variegated-leaf green DAMIFI." Although she seemed somewhat puzzled, she thanked me and started back to her table. Since my conscience bothered me, I stopped her and explained that I really didn't know and that I was only "funning" her. After a good laugh, when I told her about my rather widespread use of the term DAMIFI, we both returned to our tables. Since her table was not too far distant from ours, I couldn't help overhearing her explanation to her dinner companions about her DAMIFI experience.

Later, on her way out from dinner with her companions, she stopped at our table and thanked me, stating that my little touch of humor and refreshing honesty had "MADE HER DAY!"

A Computer Problem in Heaven?

During my wife's surgical hospitalization in Atlanta, I had occasion to attend church services at the Sacred Heart Church in downtown Atlanta. Afterward, as I strolled back toward my hotel up Peachtree Street, I was quite aware of the lack of pedestrain traffic and was really shocked when I heard a mechanical-sounding voice apparently addressing me,

"EDWARD FANDT, DO NOT BE FRIGHTENED. THIS IS THE VOICE OF THE PRAYER COMPUTER IN HEAVEN, ASKING FOR YOUR HELP WITH A PROBLEM THAT CONFRONTS US. WHEN YOUR WIFE, MARY, ENTERED THE HOSPITAL, THE YELLOW ALERT SIGNAL ON THE PRAYER COMPUTER WAS ACTIVATED AND, IN TURN, AFTER SEARCHING FOR THE RIGHT RELIGIOUS DEMONINATION, ASSIGNED HER TO THE CATHOLIC PRAYER EVALUATION SECTOR FOR ANALYSIS, INTERPRETATION, AND VALUE ASSIGNMENT OF NUMERICAL EQUIVALENCIES.

THIS WORKED OUT VERY WELL AND THE COMPUTER READ-OUTS WERE ALL SIGNIFICANTLY HIGH!

HOWEVER, THERE HAS BEEN A TOTAL BLACKOUT IN THE NON-CATHOLIC SECTOR DUE TO A TORRENTIAL FLOOD OF PRAYERS FROM VARIOUS PROTESTANT, JEWISH, ISLMAIC AND OTHER NON-RELIGIOUS GROUPS THROUGHOUT EASTERN AND SOUTHERN UNITED STATES!

PLEASE—CAN YOU EXPLAIN WHY THIS SITUATION HAS DEVELOPED?"

After momentary thought, an explanation was really quite easy, so I replied, "Mary is a Catholic and has many Catholic friends who are rooting for her in this present crisis but since some 82 percent of the friends that we have made during our forty-five years of marriage are non-Catholics and most of them have such love and high respect for her, there has been a spontaneous outpouring of prayers, hopes and best wishes for a speedy recovery! Viva, those friends who really care!"

"VERY POSSIBLE! THANK YOU!"

On my next walking trip back from the church a few days later, I listened carefully—but there was no further communication, so I assumed that everything had been resolved.

This is not meant to be derogatory or in any way even sacrilegious! It is written as a most sincere tribute and "thank you" to our many friends, to church and religious groups throughout the world who have offered prayers for Mary, and to non-affiliated persons who have expressed their hopes for a speedy recovery—with the total net result to date that "There is wonderful progress!"

My Turn in the Barrel!

After six years of successfully avoiding hospitalization in South Carolina, events finally caught up with me on Father's Day in June, 1985, as we officially began our seventh year of gracious Southern living. During the preceeding weeks, I had been forced to visit our local doctor several times to remedy a bronchial asthma situation which left me gasping for breath. The usual procedure consisted of shots of epinephrine and adrenaline, followed by rest and relaxation for several hours. This time, however, there was no relief and even repeating the procedure the following day still left me barely able to breathe.

Accordingly, I was consigned to the local hospital and sent to the Intensive Care Unit for total monitoring and reinforced continuous medication, supplemented with respiratory therapy.

Back in March, during one of my problem sessions, the doctor had teased me about his report in which he had written down in the complaint section, "S.O.B.," and explained that he was not really characterizing me but just indicating that it was a shortness of breath that was associated with my problem.

After twenty-four hours in I.C.U., during which some activity, medication, or therapy took place at least every two hours, I was pronounced to be improving. I was released to a private room and the varied activities were shifted to a four-hour basis—but here, at least, the beds were six feet long and I could finally unfold my legs. After the second day in a private room, my lungs seemed to be nearly cleared of wheezing and I was advised that I would probably be allowed to be discharged if I was able to cope successfully with a computerized respiratory testing and evaluation program on the following morning. (I stayed awake most of the night, practicing holding my breath and inhaling and exhaling both slowly and rapidly.)

On the day of the test, I was introduced to the computerized machine and had the various aspects of the evaluation and graphing explained to me. It took approximately an hour to complete the program and to complete the profile of my breathing patterns in varied situations. Inquiries as to just what was disclosed concerning my breathing patterns still left me wondering—the graphs were interesting and the numerical data, I suppose, might have some value.

Having "wasted" the morning with the test, I decided that I might as well have some enjoyment and proceeded to discuss with the respiratory technician certain aspects of the test which impinged on the validity of the results—1. the fact that my dentures were loose during the tests and I could not control the air totally during the various blowing exercises, especially the one dealing with blowing up the balloon; 2. the test was strictly predicated upon the testee being a "mouth-breather," but since I am a snorer, I have been rather forcefully conditioned to becoming a "nose-breather" during some forty-five years of marital bliss. Hence, in my humble opinion, I could not place too much credence in the results.

The lovely young lady technician listened carefully and pondered the points that I had brought to her attention. Thoughtfully she asked me, "Are you really sure just what you doctor meant when he used the abbreviated term S.O.B.—was it under complaint, diagnosis, or personal evaluation? The test is completed—you may leave . . . NOW!"

Certain Books Can Be Hazardous to Your Health!

When the local bookmobile delivered *Love and War* by John Jakes, as per my request, I was rather awed by its size (six and one-half inches by nine and one-half inches by two and one-half inches thick) and by the number of pages (1019).

I tackled the book (I usually read in bed) but had a problem holding the book up because of its size and weight. The next morning I complained that the muscles in my arms ached because of the size and weight of the book. So—I decided to actually weigh the book on our bathroom scale, but since I couln't get an accurate measurement, I ended up weighing myself both holding the book and without the book. The net result was a difference of four pounds! However, since there was some question as to the accuracy of the electronic digital scale, I then proceeded to weigh the book on our kitchen scale. Since the range of this scale was two pounds, I ended up weighing the book twice and determined that the book really did weigh four pounds!

The next night, due to my aching arms, I propped up a pillow to hold the book upright while I was reading. I fell asleep, however, and woke up "fighting for survival" since the book had fallen on my chest and the pillow was covering my nose and mouth. Yes, I survived!

The following evening, I sat up in a chair in the living room to read, holding the book in my lap. All went well until I fell asleep and the book slid off my lap and fell on my right foot, severely bruising three toes. Disgusted, I went to bed, placing the book on the floor beside my bed. During the night, I had occasion to go to the bathroom and when I stepped down on the floor, I twisted my left ankle since, unfortunately, I stepped down on the book instead of the floor!

Yes, eventually I did finish the book—but it was most certainly hazardous to my physical health!

Next, I tried some books of a different nature.

First, I attempted *Aztec* by Gary Jennings (a long-winded chronicle as told by an elderly male Indian of the Aztec tribe). I struggled through interminable pages of unpronouncable names, places and events, highlighted only by the explicit accounts of his incestuous relationship with his sister and the detailed sexual operations of the princess to whom he was in bondage. Since I was bored, I fell asleep and later, gave up on this book.

Then I tried *Chesapeake* by James Michener, since I had lived for a year in and traveled rather extensively through the areas of Maryland and Virginia that were highlighted in this story. Once again, Michener's typical long-winded, ultra-descriptive style soon lulled me to sleep. Eventually, I did manage to finish the book, weeks later.

Finally, in desperation, I started to read *Passions* by Barney Leason but found that, although there were implied sexual overtones to the story, the reader soon became bored with page after page of precise picayune descriptions of every item of wearing apparel and the room decor, with lengthy dissertations on the background of even the minor characters involved in the story. Again, I slept more than I read!

The focus of the problem related in this section has to do with the fact that when I am bored with a book, I tend to fall into deep slumber and then I SNORE! I never realized how really horrible my snoring was until my daughters, in desperation, taped me snoring and then played it back to me. While now there is only my wife to listen to the sounds of my snoring, I know how upset she gets (and rightly so!). Hence, I tend to classify boring books as being hazardous to continued marital happiness!

For a change of pace, I then tried *Chances* by Jackie Collins, a national best seller. This was one of the filthiest books that I have ever read! You may assume that I have led a most sheltered life, but that is not so. Oh, I didn't fall asleep—but the explicit, rampant sexual activities which were covered in lurid detail left the reader somewhat nauseated and disgusted since there was nothing left to the imagination!

This type of book I classify as being hazardous to my sound emotional health and continued connubial bliss!

After discussing some of these problems with several of

our friends during the bi-weekly coffee klatch after the visit of the county bookmobile, one of our friends volunteered another, almost-tragic problem relating to the topic, that he had become aware of.

A friend of his has a serious sight problem—to the extent that his reading material is mostly magazines and books that are printed in Braille. This friend burned his finger tips while picking up a hot popcorn popper just shortly before his Braille-edition of Playboy arrived. Can you imagine his mental state while he was forced to wait an entire week until his finger tips healed so that he could finally "read" the centerfold of the issue?

Who Was That Masked Man?

If this question had been asked back in the semi-early days of television, in all probability the answer might have been The Lone Ranger, Zorro, Batman, or the Green Hornet—masked persons who were dedicated to rescuing the downtrodden and oppressed!

Unfortunately, today many of our senior citizens who have been exposed to hospitalization and operations can only envision green-masked medical personnel as being a major (and expensive) factor in their lives. Since this personnel often serves in supportive roles or provides supplementary services, the patient may never even meet them and really becomes aware of them through the medium of charges and billings that are submitted.

Since I may have occasion to be further exposed to these specialists and/or technicians personally in the days and years ahead, I am not even attempting to criticize their charges as being "generally exorbitant or excessive"!

When the politicians and governmental sages began to become involved in the rising medical costs and attempted to devise ways to control these costs, a new, anonomyous clerical bureaucracy was created in both the Medicare and Medicaid Agencies that made decisions and monetary approvals on all of the billings going through these organizations. Without going through all of the details of the processes by which these clerical personnel determine "customary charges," "prevailing charges," "allowable percentage of increase," and so on, I assure you that it is most enlightening if you attempt to appeal any of their decisions.

I have been frustrated over the past four years as I have attempted to question or appeal the decisions of this anonymous clerical bureaucracy because in most instances it is impossible to even find the initials or any clue to the decision maker's name or identity.

Thus, unless you are fortunate to have a doctor or a medical technician who will "accept assignment"—think twice before you condemn someone who apparently charges two to three times the prevailing rate for services or who appears to waste funds for additional x-rays or tests in order to protect himself from the huge malpractice suits that are so common in today's world. Perhaps the real "masked robber" is the semi-trained clerical personnel who are allowed to make cost decisions on medical problems that are beyond their comprehension or knowledge!

Why do I focus on this problem? Frankly, health care and health problems are of primary concern to most retired persons. A recent survey indicated that elderly Americans currently spend some 15 percent of their income on health care costs, with higher percentages projected for the years ahead.

"As time goes by", most of us are bound to be faced with various medical problems—some of short duration, others of a more serious nature. There is no panacea that applies to any and all situations as we have found out as we "learned" patiently to walk; to breathe; to swallow; to eat; to talk *again,* following various operations and medical care.

We attempt to "think positive" and to "just take it one day at a time"! Plus, my wife and I make it a ritual to hold hands and after we have said GRACE every Sunday morning, repeat together with emphasis, "We made it through another week!" Come join with us!

The Difference between Men and Boys Is Basically the Cost of Their Toys!

About a year ago, when I faced the reality of declining income from interest-bearing investments and higher tax costs due to the taxation of half of our Social Security benefits, it became obvious that a new source of supplemental income must be developed. After considerable thought, I decided to attempt to combine some of the various stories and incidents that I had written up and distributed to friends into a salable compilation of stories and attempt to locate a publisher who would be willing to try to market the product.

After discussing the situation with my two daughters and my son-in-law and with several close friends—all of whom encouraged me to make the effort—I began to investigate the home computer market for up-to-date tools to utilize in my efforts. Eventually I purchased an Apple 11C computer and imagewriter and began a self-tutorial program of instruction.

Our younger daughter and her husband were most helpful to me in these efforts since they already owned one and were very familiar with the Apple 11 system and programs. Some nine months later, I feel quite as ease with my "toy" and have adapted it for correspondence, financial records, and especially for writing my stories or vignettes.

The title of this section, "The Difference between Men and Boys is Basically the Cost of Their Toys," really is a quotation from a letter from a dear friend who, perhaps, doubts the seriousness of my purpose and assumes that it is only a toy to keep me occupied and out of trouble. (After all, who has ever heard of an almost sixty-nine–year–old man attempting to write his first book?). Since she may be correct in her assumption, I cannot dare to criticize until the evidence is all in and the total cost of my toy and its operation is compiled.

In the meantime, I have learned a new skill and, each day, add to my knowledge of computer operation. Also, since I am no longer allowed to smoke, my hands are gainfully occupied and there is no time available for cigarettes or alcoholic beverage consumption. Good therapy!

When I was considering the purchase of the computer, the manager of the sales center, after determining that I did not plan to spend seventy-five dollars for an instructional course on the use of the computer, suggested as follows: "Remember that computers don't BYTE" (a computer term meaning a sequence of eight bits that represent an instruction, a letter, a number, or a punctuation mark). Also, "The unbridled terror and fear of computers is known as Cyberphobia. To prevent this happening to you, make friends with your computer by giving it a name (obscene names don't count)."

Now you know why I refer to my Apple computer as "EVE"!

The Big Cola Debate

During the current year we have had maximum exposure from the media and advertising, featuring the merits of both Coco-Cola and Pepsi-Cola as each company attempted to improve its marketing position. Coco-Cola even capitulated to its customers by returning the "old Coke" to the marketplace. In the meantime, the screaming rock star commercials from both companies assaulted your eardrums!

The Cola Debate referred to in this story is probably mostly of interest to retired folks and deals with the C.O.L.A. (cost of living adjustments) to Social Security. The various members of Congress have made overtures to the retired segment of the population in order to secure voting power in the future elections by promising again and again that "Social Security benefits will never be reduced or subjected to taxes".

It's the same old song that has been heard over and over as these lawmakers are seeking solutions to the budgetary crisis that has in the past and continues to be one of the major problems faced by the pork-barrel and log-rolling representatives of our democractic form of government.

Past efforts have resulted in shiftings and delays in the cost of living adjustments—much to the chagrin of many Social Security recipients who, in the belief that the government will take care of them from the cradle to the grave, just cannot manage in a society that places the poverty level at a figure that is beginning to approach the twenty-thousand figure.

As this is being written, the debate still is unresolved, as is the final adoption of a fiscal budget for the U.S. government for the ensuing year. There were long vacations for congressional members, jaunts for many of them, together with family, staff and friends to far-off world centers to evaluate situations, local fund-raising dinners and politicking for the future years— really vital issues if one is interested in continuing in Congress and enjoying the various "perks" associated with this arduous life.

And the retired persons continue to ask, "Will there be a C.O.L.A. this year and, if so, will it be deferred again or, possibly, subjected to a means test of some kind?"

A rather caustic friend of mine insists that if we are going to be, "subjected to fornication again, this time he would at least like to be kissed"!

Just one week later this friend stopped at the house and reopened the topic with this remark: "Ed, I've changed my mind about the cola problem. After reading about AIDS and then hearing on the TV about how they arrested this fellow who had AIDS and charged him with assault with a deadly weapon because he spit on several policeman—I don't even want to be *kissed!*"

Changes in Our Life-style

Reflections on the changes in our life-style during the past ten years indicate both concern for the feeling of others and the changing health implications of some of our friends and ourselves.

Prior to retirement, as we traveled to visit friends, it was rather customary to bring along as a gift, a bottle of our favorite bourbon, Ancient Age, plus either wine, candy or fruit.

After retirement, since it seemed that we are mostly visiting retired folks, the connotation of "ancient age" really bothered us—so, as a visitation gift we began to bring along a bottle which we felt was reflective of our life style, Southern Comfort.

Then, as we faced the reality that most of our friends that we were visiting no longer either smoked or consumed alcholic beverages, it really became a question of which fruit or diet soft drink might be most appropriate.

It used to be a distinct pleasure to go out-and-around for dinner and, as we have traversed some thirty-five states on our various trips and adventures, we have complied a list of many dining places that we and our friends might enjoy.

Recently, due to medical problems, we have been limited in the digestible cuisine area and, in addition, have encountered a sight problem which makes night driving a real problem. Hence, a daytime luncheon outing has become our acceptable substitute. We still tease the waitresses and complain that, since they didn't cover the carafe of wine, it's their fault because it evaporated! Most of these girls greet us when we return because they think that Mary is a real martyr for putting up with me—and they do like the twenty-percent tip that Mary insists on!

Our two daughters—neither of whom smoke—have carried on a relentless crusade for the past eighteen years to convince Mary and me to give up smoking since it is so injurious to our health!

While both of us have made spasmodic efforts over the years and have never smoked in either of their homes, it has not been an easy battle for either of us. During our visitations to their homes, we just went outside and smoked on the porch areas and managed to survive.

Since the advent of Mary's intraoral cancer and the follow-up operation, she has been adamant about never smoking again—and after my asthma problem, joined forces with my doctors to coerce me into joining her in the non-smoking segment of living humanity!

Yes indeed! There have been changes in our life-style! But . . . since we are alive and well, who really misses those pitchers of Manhattans at 8:00 A.M. before the bicycle races; the "bloody Marys" before the early-morning Lion's Club Convention meetings; the all-night sessions at the state American Legion Conventions; the long-winded cocktail hours and dinners of the local and state education groups and federated boards of education. . . ?

WE DO!

Thank You!

I appreciate your interest in reading my efforts or at least in reaching this point in the publication!

While we all have diverse viewpoints and different ways of expressing ourselves, I am always interested in constructive criticisms and suggestions since it is my firm intention—unless this is a complete flop—to complete a somewhat complementary publication which will focus on some of the housing situations, vacations, confidence scams, and similar problem that retired folks are exposed to.

Although I cannot promise to answer all letters and suggestions that may be sent to me, I will read and give consideration to all positive criticisms and suggestions!

Edward L. Fandt
Rt. 2, Box 127
Starr, SC 29684